CW01643050

Table of Con...

Introduction - What if your life had an invisible thread?

Why do some people seem to be filled with simple joy, clear direction and unshakeable inner peace? Their lives are not necessarily easy or perfect. But they move forward with a sense of coherence, meaning and rightness. Perhaps that is what living your **Ikigai** is all about.

This Japanese word, which has become popular around the world, literally means **"reason for being"**, or more precisely: **"that which makes life worth living every day"**.

Contrary to popular belief, Ikigai is **not a goal to be achieved**, nor is it an exceptional mission or a "dream job". It is **a path, a way of living in the present** with presence, joy and consistency. It can be found in the smallest everyday gestures as well as in major life choices. It can evolve. Transform. And even be reborn from your greatest pains.

What you will discover in this guide

This book offers a journey in **50 concrete**, structured and accessible **sections** to help you:

- Understand what Ikigai really is (and what it is not)
- Take stock of yourself: your strengths, desires, values, needs
- Articulate the four dimensions of Ikigai (passion, mission, profession, vocation)
- Establish routines and lifestyle choices that are aligned with your Ikigai
- Radiate your Ikigai in your relationships, your projects, your daily life

Each sheet is a **practical key** to **help you move forward step by step**, at your own pace, without dogma or miracle solutions. You can read this guide in order or pick and choose according to your needs at the time.

Why not start today?

You don't need to change everything, know everything or understand everything to get started. All it takes is one step. One impulse. One choice.

This book is not here to tell you **what to do**, but to help you **feel what resonates within you**. It will not impose anything on you. It will invite you to find yourself.

Ready to walk the path of your Ikigai? Then open the first page... and embark on an inner journey that could transform your outlook on life.

About the author – Laurent Vigne

Laurent Vigne is passionate about life paths that combine meaning, simplicity and inner transformation. For more than 15 years, he has been exploring personal development practices, Eastern philosophies, humanistic psychology and concrete methods for better living.

Over the years, he has helped many people **reconnect with what truly motivates them**, whether in their personal lives, their professional activities or their daily choices.

Through this book, he shares an accessible, lively and guilt-free vision of Ikigai, far from the injunctions to "succeed in life" and close to the essential: **loving to be alive**.

Part 1 - Understanding Ikigai deeply

SHEET 1 – The Japanese origins of Ikigai

Ancient wisdom from Japan

The word **Ikigai** is made up of two elements:

- **"Iki" (生き)**, which means "to live"
- **"Gai" (甲斐)**, which refers to value, reason, the fruit of effort

In other words, **Ikigai** literally means *"that which makes life worth living."*
This is not a theoretical concept, but a **philosophy lived out on a daily basis** in Japanese culture. Ikigai is not reserved for monks or philosophers, but is an integral part of the way of life for many people, particularly in the Okinawa region, famous for the exceptional longevity of its inhabitants.

It is only recently that the term has crossed borders and been popularised in the West thanks to books such as *Ikigai: The Japanese Secret to a Long and Happy Life*. Unfortunately, this popularity has also simplified and even distorted the concept.

More than a goal: a way of being

In Japanese tradition, **Ikigai is not a goal to be achieved**. It is not a grand project or a single mission. Rather, it is **a subtle and intimate dynamic** that connects what we love, what we do, and how that fits into the world.

It can be embodied in:

- A well-tended garden
- A carefully shared tea ritual
- A caring presence for the elderly
- A craft practised day after day with love

For the Japanese, Ikigai **does not need to be profitable or recognised**. It can be discreet, invisible to others, but deeply alive within oneself. All it needs to do is give **a feeling of intimate satisfaction**, a peaceful joy upon waking, a simple motivation to get up in the morning.

The West has transformed it... sometimes wrongly

When the concept arrived in Europe and the United States, it was often summarised in a **diagram with four circles**:

What I love

What I am good at

What I can be paid for

What the world needs

This diagram is useful, but it **only reflects part** of the original essence of Ikigai. It tends to:

- Overemphasise the professional or paid aspect
- Create pressure to "succeed" or "achieve"
- Overlook the simple, everyday dimension rooted in being

It is therefore essential to return to **the cultural roots** of this concept: a **way of life**, rather than a career goal.

What you can take away from this

- Ikigai is a **quiet joy of living**, born of small, aligned actions
- It does not depend **on money** or external recognition
- It **is not fixed**: it can change with the seasons of your life
- It is often expressed in simplicity: what you love to do, what you do well, what connects you to others

Practical exercise

Take a few minutes to answer, without looking for the "right" answer:

1. What little things bring me joy every day?
2. When I feel fully alive, what am I doing?
3. What action or activity makes me want to get up in the morning?

You may have just discovered a **spark of Ikigai**.

SHEET 2 – The true meaning of the word Ikigai

Ikigai is a Japanese word often translated as "reason for being" or "what gives meaning to life". But this translation is far too simplistic. The true meaning of the word Ikigai is **more subtle, more intimate, more alive**. It refers to that sometimes subtle but powerful feeling of having a good reason to get up in the morning.

Ikigai does not refer to an abstract idea or a grandiose mission. It refers to **the personal experience of a meaningful life**, a connection between who you are, what you do and what you bring to the world, even on a small scale. It can be visible or invisible, professional or non-professional, social or intimate.

In Japanese, **Iki** means "to live" and **Gai** refers to value, interest or benefit. Ikigai is therefore **the value we find in our own lives**, in our activities, relationships and development. It is what makes life "worth living", not in a solemn way, but in the simplicity of everyday life.

A concept that is lived rather than thought

One of the pitfalls of the Western approach is to want **to intellectualise** Ikigai, as if it were a problem to be solved. We search for our Ikigai as we would search for a destination, a life goal, a single key. But in Japan, Ikigai is seen more as a **natural process**, a thread of life that is revealed by being fully present to oneself, to the world and to others.

You don't "find" your Ikigai once and for all. You **feel** it, you **cultivate** it, you **let** it **evolve**. It manifests itself in moments when you feel that what you are doing is right, aligned, nourishing. It can change with the stages of life, the trials you go through, and personal discoveries.

A person can have **several Ikigai** at different times: one Ikigai related to their job, another to their family, another to a passion, a commitment, a garden, an artistic or spiritual practice. Ikigai is alive. It breathes.

Freeing yourself from the pressure of finding "great meaning"

Many people search for their Ikigai as one might search for true love or an existential Holy Grail. This can become a source of stress, comparison, and even feelings of failure. But this is the opposite of the spirit of Ikigai.

True Ikigai does not require you to be exceptional. It invites you to be **fully yourself**. It is not there to flatter your ego, but to **anchor your life in the present**, with clarity and consistency. It reconnects you to what makes you feel good, to what is meaningful to you, **even if no one else notices**.

Reflections to write down in a notebook

- What activities or situations make me lose track of time?
- What gives me a sense of contribution, of usefulness, even if it is modest?

- If I didn't have anything to prove to anyone, what would I do every day with joy?

Take the time to write freely, without censoring yourself. Ikigai often reveals itself **in what we neglect or underestimate**. An old passion. A simple habit. A gesture that reconnects you.

SHEET 3 – Ikigai is not found, it is built

We often hear the injunction: *"Find your Ikigai!"* As if it were a hidden treasure, an inner secret to be discovered once and for all. But this view is misleading. It gives the illusion that Ikigai is a fixed entity, a destination to be reached or a truth that is already there, that all you have to do is "find" it.

In reality, **Ikigai is a living process, a personal, evolving construction**. It is shaped as we move through life, through our experiences, our trials, our mistakes, our joys, our questioning. It is not given. It is cultivated.

That's why there's no point in waiting for a sudden revelation. Ikigai is built **through action**, **through self-awareness**, **through the gradual adjustment** between what you love, what you know how to do, what makes you feel good, and what you want to offer the world.

The myth of the perfect moment

Waiting to "find your Ikigai" before changing your life is often a disguised excuse: we wait until everything is clear before taking action. But the opposite is true: **by acting, testing, and exploring**, we gradually clarify what really suits us.

There is **no ideal moment**, no perfect situation. It is in reality, in your current daily life, in your present constraints, that you can begin to build a more aligned lifestyle. By changing a habit. By making more room for an activity that nourishes you. By saying yes to a desire you had been suppressing.

Ikigai is not a leap into the void, but **a path of small steps**.

The logic of life

Thinking of Ikigai as a construction means viewing it **as a living organism**, not as an equation to be solved. It grows with you. It responds to you. It can change shape without losing its essence. It can even transform completely after a shock, a bereavement, or a realisation.

Sometimes, a vocation that we thought we had found ceases to nourish us. This is not a failure. It is **a sign of evolution**. It is then time to adjust, re-evaluate and reformulate your Ikigai. This flexibility is a strength.

In practice: how can you build it on a daily basis?

- By **trying** out new activities or routines that appeal to you
- By **listening to your feelings** after each experience: fatigue or enthusiasm? Frustration or joy?
- By **noting down your intuitions and insights** in a personal notebook
- By **talking to people who inspire you** and observing what resonates with you
- By **giving things time**, without trying to rush things

Journal – Guided reflection

Take a notebook and answer this question: **What activities in my daily life give me real satisfaction (even if they seem mundane or unimportant)?**

Then complete this sentence every day for a week: **Today, I felt a sense of meaning in...**

After a few days, you will begin to see a **common thread** emerge. This is what you can follow and reinforce. Your Ikigai is built from this subtle thread.

SHEET 4 – The 4 circles of Ikigai: passion, mission, profession, vocation

One of the best-known diagrams of Ikigai in the West is that of **four intersecting circles**, at the centre of which lies your Ikigai. This model has been very successful because it offers a simple method for reflecting on your life. It is not perfect (we will look at its limitations later), but it can be a **good starting point** for exploring your personal balance.

The four circles represent:

1. **What you enjoy doing**
2. **What you are good at**
3. **What you can be paid for**
4. **What the world needs**

When these four dimensions align, it is said that you are at the heart of your Ikigai. It is a state where **joy, skill, usefulness and contribution come together**.

Decoding the four dimensions

1. What you love
This is what excites you, what makes you lose track of time. It is the emotional driving force. If you had to do one activity every day without obligation, this would be it. It can be creative, manual, intellectual, relational...

2. What you are good at

These are your natural or acquired talents. It's less about qualifications and more about real, visible, useful skills. It could be your ease of communication, your problem-solving ability, your organisational skills, etc.

3. What you can get paid for

This is the professional dimension. It corresponds to what the market recognises as useful and marketable. It requires you to adapt to reality and make concrete choices: how can you turn a passion or skill into a viable business?

4. What the world needs

This is the contribution dimension. It calls on your sense of service, commitment, and social or environmental usefulness. It reconnects your individual journey to a broader reality.

When the circles overlap

- **Passion** = What you love + What you are good at
- **Mission** = What you love + What the world needs
- **Profession** = What you are good at + What you can be paid for
- **Vocation** = What the world needs + What you can get paid for

These areas of overlap show that you can already **live out parts of your Ikigai**, even if all the circles are not yet joined.

Limitations of the model

This diagram is **useful but incomplete**. It gives the impression that you must necessarily bring all four circles together to live your Ikigai. However, many people find meaning in their lives **without it being related to their profession**. Others live their Ikigai through simple or voluntary activities.

Furthermore, this model emphasises **usefulness and profitability**, which is not true to the Japanese spirit of Ikigai, which is more focused on **joie de vivre, presence and simplicity**.

Practical exercise

On a sheet of paper, draw four circles and start filling each area with your own elements:

- What I enjoy doing:
- What I am good at:
- What I could be paid for:
- What I think the world needs:

Don't try to fill everything in perfectly. Leave some areas blank. The important thing is to **make an initial map of your inner territory**. This diagram will evolve with you.

SHEET 5 – Why this model is incomplete (and what to do instead)

The famous Ikigai diagram with its four circles has become a benchmark tool in personal development. It is often presented as the royal road to a balanced life. However, this model is **a Western creation**, inspired by Japanese ideas but greatly simplified. It reflects **neither authentic Japanese culture** nor the true richness of the Ikigai experience.

This fact sheet aims to **kindly deconstruct** the limitations of this diagram and offer a more vibrant alternative that is more faithful to the original spirit.

The main limitations of the 4-circle model

1. It creates pressure to be perfect
This model assumes that in order to achieve one's Ikigai, one must tick all four boxes: love, be competent, be paid, and be useful to the world. But few people tick all four simultaneously, and this can lead to discouragement or a feeling of failure.

2. It promotes a productivist vision
By emphasising monetisability and usefulness, this model aligns Ikigai with a logic of profitability. However, Ikigai can exist in things that are free, useless in the eyes of the world, but deeply nourishing internally.

3. It overlooks temporality
Ikigai is not fixed. It evolves with age, life circumstances

and events. This model gives the illusion of a fixed goal to be achieved, as if once you have found it, everything is settled.

4. It does not take into account the being

This model remains focused on doing (activities, employment, missions), whereas authentic Ikigai also includes states of being: joy, peace, presence, connection to oneself and others.

A more accurate approach: Ikigai as a vibration

What if we stopped looking for Ikigai as an external target? What if, instead, we listened to it as an **inner vibration**?

Rather than asking questions like "What should I do?", it may be more accurate to ask:

- What makes me feel alive?
- What brings me deep peace?
- What connects me to others, without effort or sacrifice?
- What would I do again even if I wasn't paid for it?

This attitude changes everything. It **reconnects Ikigai to the quality of presence** we bring to what we do, rather than the results we get from it.

Building a fluid Ikigai, day after day

Abandoning rigid patterns does not mean giving up all structure. It means choosing a more lively, more flexible model. Here is a simple alternative:

1. What gives me energy
2. What is meaningful to me
3. What I want to express to the world
4. What I am willing to nurture consistently

At the intersection of these four axes, you can build **your own personal Ikigai path**, one that is constantly evolving and resonates with your needs, values and impulses of the moment.

An invitation to explore differently

Close your eyes for a moment. Let a recent memory come to mind where you felt completely yourself. What were you doing? With whom? What was your state of mind? How did your body feel?

Write down this memory in detail. It may contain **a living key to your Ikigai**, much more valuable than an abstract model.

SHEET 6 – Ikigai and joie de vivre: a key to everyday life

Ikigai is sometimes presented as an existential quest, a grand life project, or even an almost spiritual mission. But in its simplest and most authentic form, Ikigai is above all a **daily source of joie de vivre**, a little spark that makes you want to get up in the morning, even without any spectacular reason.

This joie de vivre is not a passing pleasure or fleeting excitement. It is a **deep and stable joy**, often discreet, rooted in the coherence between who you are, what you do, and how you feel. It is what connects you to yourself, to others, to life.

Joy is not a luxury: it is a signal

Society often values effort, success, and productivity. Joy, on the other hand, is often relegated to the status of a bonus or reward. However, in the Ikigai approach, **joy is a fundamental signal**. It tells you that you are on the right path, that what you are doing is in tune with your true nature.

It is not a boisterous joy. It is a **quiet joy**, a feeling of fluidity, of inner lightness. A kind of momentum without logical reason, but which makes you want to be there, fully.

Living your Ikigai means **nurturing this joy regularly**, honouring it, listening to it, even on ordinary or difficult days.

Cultivating joy through small things

Many people think their lives are not special enough to talk about Ikigai. Yet **it is often the simplest gestures that nourish this joy the most**:

- Taking the time to cook a dish you love
- Walking in silence in nature
- Reading, writing, creating
- Listening to someone with presence
- Offering a service, a smile, a kind word

Ikigai does not always lie in big projects, but in those moments when **you are aligned, sincere, alive**. The more attention you pay to these moments, the more you strengthen your connection to your Ikigai.

Avoid two pitfalls: expectation and perfection

The first pitfall is believing that Ikigai must resemble a clear, well-defined, useful and profitable vocation. This expectation creates pressure and confusion, and distances you from your feelings.

The second pitfall is seeking a perfect form of joy: always intense, always clear. But the joy associated with Ikigai is often **modest, stable, and gentle** . It doesn't shout. It doesn't impose itself. It is felt. It lives within you.

Don't look for fireworks. Look for an inner flame, calm but constant.

Practical exercise

At the end of each day this week, write down in a notebook:

1. A moment when you felt simple joy
2. What you were doing
3. What it says about you, your needs, your impulses

After a few days, reread your notes. You will see **recurring patterns** emerge, concrete signs of what nourishes your Ikigai. This is where you can move forward.

SHEET 7 – What Ikigai is not

To truly live your Ikigai, it is important to **make room for what it really is**, but also to **free yourself from the misconceptions** associated with it. In the West, the word "Ikigai" has been taken up, amplified, and sometimes stripped of its depth. By trying to turn it into a miracle method or career plan, we risk missing out on its true richness.

In this article, we will clarify **what Ikigai is not**, in order to avoid the frequent confusion that slows down momentum or creates frustration.

Ikigai is not an ideal job

Contrary to popular belief, Ikigai **is not necessarily a profession**. It does not necessarily involve changing careers, retraining or becoming an entrepreneur. Of course, for some people, it may be expressed through their work. But for others, it manifests itself **outside of any paid activity**: in volunteer work, in a creative passion, in caring for a loved one, in a personal journey.

Thinking that Ikigai must be profitable or visible can create unnecessary pressure. It cuts you off from what you are already experiencing, here and now, which could be a very accurate expression of your Ikigai.

Ikigai is not a sudden revelation

Ikigai is not a truth that you discover all at once, like a sudden calling. There isn't necessarily a magical moment when everything becomes clear. Most of the time, **Ikigai emerges gradually,** as you listen to your feelings, explore your desires and adjust your choices. It is a **process of refinement** rather than a flash of genius.

Waiting for a perfect revelation often delays action and experience. But it is **through living that Ikigai reveals itself**.

Ikigai is not a call to performance.

Searching for your Ikigai should not become another pressure to "succeed in life". It is not a race for productivity, nor a means of distinguishing yourself or proving your worth. It is the opposite: a return to the essentials, **to the pleasure of existing and contributing to the best of your ability**.

Ikigai does not require you to be perfect, competent or constantly useful. It also welcomes breaks, doubts and trial and error. It makes room for the human, not just the optimised.

Ikigai is not reserved for an elite few

You don't have to be an artist, therapist, coach, monk or world traveller to have an Ikigai. It is not reserved for those who have time, money or a high level of consciousness. It can be experienced in **any life**, through simple gestures, an attitude, a presence.

It is this universality that makes Ikigai so precious. It belongs to everyone, regardless of their situation.

Reflection to note in a notebook

Complete this sentence every day for a week:

"Today, I was fully myself when..."

You will see that it is not about great achievements, but about ordinary, real moments that touch your truth. These moments show you **where your Ikigai already exists.**

SHEET 8 – The difference between Ikigai, flow and happiness

In the field of personal development, several concepts seem to be similar: **Ikigai, flow,** happiness... However, these notions do not refer **to the same thing** or the same experiences. Confusing them can lead to unrealistic expectations or even misunderstandings about what we are really looking for.

The purpose of this sheet is to clarify these differences so that you can recognise what you are experiencing — without straying from your path or priorities.

Ikigai: a guiding principle, not an emotion

Ikigai is above all **a personal meaning given to life**. It is not a passing emotion or an exceptional state of consciousness. It is a way of being, **a axis of coherence**, an inner direction that connects what you love, what drives you, what you want to offer to the world.

You could say that Ikigai is **the overall framework**, the underlying driving force, sometimes discreet but always stable. It is not always joyful, but it is **deeply nourishing**. You can live your Ikigai even when you are tired or facing challenges, as long as you feel that what you are doing is meaningful to you.

Flow: a state of intense experience

Flow is a term from positive psychology, popularised by Mihaly Csikszentmihalyi. It refers to a **state of total immersion** in an activity: maximum concentration, loss of sense of time, feeling of fluid efficiency. You can experience flow when writing, painting, teaching, coding, playing an instrument...

Flow is **temporary** and linked to a specific activity. It provides **intense satisfaction** in the moment, but says nothing about your life as a whole. You can experience states of flow while feeling a general loss of meaning — and vice versa.

Happiness: emotional balance

Happiness is a broad term, often used incorrectly. It can refer to a state of joy, satisfaction, inner peace... or simply the absence of suffering. But it is often conceived as **the ultimate goal** — which can become a source of frustration, because happiness is **inherently unstable**.

Happiness depends in part on circumstances (health, relationships, environment), but also on how we interpret them. We can be happy at times without living our Ikigai, or live our Ikigai while going through periods that are not particularly "happy" but are nonetheless meaningful.

Three different, complementary keys

- **Flow** is a **vivid experience**: intense, present, localised
- **Happiness** is an **overall emotional state**, often fragile

- **Ikigai** is a **way of life**: profound, stable, vibrant

They are not interchangeable, but **feed off each other**. Your Ikigai can contain moments of flow and contribute to more lasting happiness, without confusing the two.

Guided reflection

Take the time to write down in a notebook:

1. An activity that makes me lose track of time (flow)
2. A moment when I felt deeply happy in recent months
3. Something I do regularly that gives meaning to my life, even if it is inconspicuous

By identifying these three dimensions, you will be able to better adjust your choices, recognising what truly nourishes you.

SHEET 9 – Ikigai as a way of life

What if living your Ikigai wasn't a distant goal, but a **daily practice**, like taking care of your body, your home or your garden? Rather than seeking Ikigai as a Holy Grail, it may be more accurate to consider it as a **way of life**: a set of actions, attentions and choices that nourish, day after day, a sense of coherence and vitality.

Like any hygiene, Ikigai does not need to be perfect. It is based on **regularity, awareness, adjustment** and, above all, presence of mind.

Living your Ikigai means honouring yourself every day

We sometimes take care of our appearance, our health or our efficiency, but what about what **makes** us **want to live**? What fuels our drive, our quiet joy, our sense of contribution? Living your Ikigai is not about radically changing your life, but about **recognising what makes you feel good and consciously cultivating it**.

This could be:

- Taking 20 minutes in the morning for an activity that recharges our batteries
- Saying no to things that exhaust or disconnect us
- Devoting time to a meaningful project
- Surrounding yourself with people who lift you up

- Reconnecting with a forgotten practice

The pillars of an Ikigai lifestyle

1. Inner clarity
Regularly take stock of what motivates, exhausts or nourishes you.

2. Paying attention to small, genuine pleasures
Identify what brings you simple joy in your day and make more room for it.

3. Listen to your feelings
Your body, emotions and moods are valuable indicators. Learn to read them as signals.

4. Be consistent in your actions
Align what you feel, what you think and what you do as much as possible.

5. Constant adjustment
Ikigai is not fixed. It evolves with you. It requires flexibility, listening, and acceptance of cycles.

Ikigai is not a performance: it is a maintenance

Just as you don't brush your teeth once and for all, you don't "find" your Ikigai and never come back to it. It is built, nurtured and readjusted. It requires **gentle attention, not pressure**. The goal is not to control everything, but to **stay alive within your own life**.

Exercise: create your Ikigai routine

Answer the following three questions in a notebook:

1. What could I do every day, even for just 5 minutes, that would reconnect me to what makes me feel good?
2. What current habit distances me from myself?
3. What small, concrete change can I make this week to honour my Ikigai more?

Choose a simple and realistic action. Start today. You have just anchored your Ikigai in your lifestyle.

SHEET 10 – What you will change by applying these sheets

Starting on the path to Ikigai is often a subtle process. It is not about dramatic changes, but rather **profound adjustments**. The changes you will make by following this book may not necessarily be visible to others. However, the effects can be powerful and lasting, transforming your life from within.

This last sheet in the first part allows you to **take stock** and become aware of what you are activating.

You will move from uncertainty to clarity

Before, you may have felt scattered, hesitant, waiting for a "trigger" or external validation. By reading and practising these sheets, you will begin to **clarify your values, your impulses, your needs**. What you really love. What you no longer want. What you need to express.

Even if everything is not yet defined, you are gaining **clarity**. And this clarity becomes an inner guide.

You will bring meaning back into the ordinary

Many people believe that you have to change your life to find meaning. In reality, Ikigai is often hidden in the everyday things we already experience but no longer notice. By applying these worksheets, you will relearn how **to see what**

is alive in your daily life: a sincere exchange, a forgotten activity, a moment of calm.

Little by little, you **will restore value to your actions, your choices, and your presence**. Meaning is not far away: it reveals itself when you are fully present.

You will act instead of waiting

The risk with big existential questions is that you can get stuck in your thinking. Here, each card invites you to **take action**, even if it's just a small step. By observing, testing and adjusting, you **become the protagonist of your Ikigai**. And this change in attitude transforms your energy.

You stop waiting for the perfect answer to move forward. You move forward, and the answer becomes clearer along the way.

You will reconnect with yourself

Applying these cards is also a return to yourself. To your feelings. To your rhythms. To your uniqueness. You stop comparing yourself. You stop trying to fit into an external model. You start **listening to what is unique to you**, what makes you tick without justification.

This reconnection may seem subtle... but it is fundamental. It is the foundation for everything else.

To anchor this change

Take a sheet of paper and complete these sentences:

- Today, I realise that what really matters to me is...
- What I am ready to change right now is...
- What I no longer want to neglect is...

Keep this sheet safe. It is your **first commitment to your living Ikigai.**

Part 2 - Getting to know yourself better in order to move forward

SHEET 11 – Identifying what makes you tick

To move towards your Ikigai, you must first learn to **recognise what touches you, moves you, and deeply inspires you**. These are not necessarily spectacular passions, but rather **sincere inner impulses**: those moments when you feel that your life is becoming more alive, more intense, more meaningful.

Identifying what makes you tick is the first step on your path to alignment. Because you can't build a meaningful life if you don't know what lights you up from within.

What excites you cannot always be explained

Sometimes a subject, activity or place attracts you for no apparent reason. It's not rational, nor is it necessarily profitable or socially acceptable. Yet you feel **something awakening within you** when you talk about it or practise it.

Do not try to justify these impulses. Welcome them as **valuable signals**. Even if they seem marginal or 'useless', they reveal an essential part of you.

Spotting the signs of inner vibration

Here are some concrete clues:

- You lose track of time when doing this activity

- You talk about it enthusiastically, even without an audience
- You feel energised after doing it
- You want to learn more about it without effort
- You feel a sense of calm, joy or inner power

These signs are unmistakable. They show that you are connected to a vibrant part of yourself. **This is where Ikigai begins to reveal itself.**

What if you don't know what makes you tick?

Many people say to themselves, "I don't know what I really like," or "I don't feel anything anymore." This can be due to habit, fatigue, overwork, or neglecting oneself. Don't panic: **the excitement will return when you seek it with gentleness, curiosity, and openness.**

Start by **revisiting what you enjoyed as a child**, or what attracted you but you never dared to do. Dare to try, without any pressure. Allow yourself time to breathe and listen.

Practical exercise

Take a sheet of paper, or better still, a notebook dedicated to your Ikigai journey.

Write down:

1. Three activities or situations in which you feel fully alive
2. Three things you would like to try if you had no constraints
3. Three memories of moments when you felt deeply at home

Reread these items several times during the week. You will see common threads emerge. These are the ones you can follow in the next worksheets.

SHEET 12 – Clarifying your natural skills

On the path to Ikigai, it is not enough to follow your desires. It is just as essential to recognise what you **can do naturally**, without excessive effort, what you are good at, even if you tend to take it for granted. These **natural skills**, whether innate or acquired, are valuable resources: they show you where your energy flows smoothly.

We often underestimate our own talents because they seem easy to us. But what is obvious to you is not necessarily obvious to others. Learning to **see your skills clearly** will allow you to better guide your choices and projects and gain confidence.

What is a natural skill?

It is an ability that comes **naturally** to you, that you exercise without effort, or that you develop very quickly when you set your mind to it. It can be technical, relational, intellectual, manual, creative...

Examples:

- You know how to listen deeply
- You are comfortable explaining things clearly
- You have an exceptional visual memory
- You have a sense of organisation or rhythm

- You are naturally comfortable with conflict or unexpected situations

These skills are not necessarily professional. But they can become **real assets** if you integrate them into your Ikigai.

Why we don't always see them

Many people think they have no talent. In reality, they are **too close to their skills to perceive them**. Like a fish in water, we no longer see what we have always been swimming in.

What's more, the education and professional systems value certain forms of intelligence (logical, linguistic) and devalue others (emotional, physical, intuitive). As a result, we think we're "not talented" because we don't fit the norm.

Clarifying your natural skills therefore also means **stepping outside of frameworks and comparisons**.

Method for identifying them

1. **Make a list of activities that you find easy and enjoyable**
    - In which you feel competent
    - That you enjoy doing, even for free
2. **Ask those around you**
    - Your family, colleagues or friends can often tell you what they admire about you, what they ask you to do

3. **Identify recurring compliments**
    - Are there qualities that people often attribute to you? "You're always calm," "You get straight to the point," "You're good at organising," etc.
4. **Remember your successes**
    - Which projects, assignments, and experiences have allowed you to excel? What resources did you use at the time?

Writing exercise

Answer these two questions in your notebook:

- What do I do well, even without thinking about it?
- If I had to teach someone something tomorrow, what could I easily pass on?

These answers will help you build the foundations of your **natural area of expertise**, an essential pillar of your Ikigai.

SHEET 13 – Explore what you can bring to the world

A living Ikigai is not solely focused on oneself. It is also rooted in **one's connection to the world, to others, and to contribution**. Even if your primary motivation comes from within, what you offer to those around you — however modest it may seem — is an **essential part of your purpose in life**.

It's not about "saving the world" or becoming indispensable. Rather, it's about **recognising your natural ability to improve, relieve, inspire, support,** clarify... in your own way. It is often in these discreet but recurring gestures that what you have come to offer takes shape.

Contributing something does not mean being visible

What you give to the world may go unnoticed, be informal, free, intimate. You can contribute:

- An atmosphere of calm
- Motivational energy
- Enlightening ideas
- Care, support, a listening ear
- Objects, texts, creations, tools

The key is that **your presence, actions, words or expertise create a positive effect**, even if subtle, around you.

Why this is important in Ikigai

When what you do **resonates beyond yourself**, it gives your actions a special depth. This connection with the outside world nurtures a **sense of usefulness** and interconnection, which strengthens the coherence between your being and your environment.

This is also what allows Ikigai to **survive moments of doubt, fatigue or crisis**: because it is not based solely on personal pleasure, but on a dynamic of sharing.

Finding your way to contribute

Ask yourself these questions:

- In what situations have I felt that my presence had a positive impact?
- Why do others naturally come to me?
- What do I convey, even without meaning to?

It may be something you already do, or **something you would like to offer but haven't dared to yet**. Don't wait for perfection: start where you are, with what you have.

Writing exercise: your footprint

Complete these sentences in your notebook:

- If I could offer the world a single message, it would be...
- If I could improve one thing around me, it would be...

- The moments when I feel truly useful are when...

Come back to these answers regularly. They are a **valuable thread** for building a life that is more aligned with what you came here to give.

SHEET 14 – Recognising what you can be paid to do

One of the key dimensions of the Ikigai framework is connecting your passions, skills and values to a concrete reality: **the possibility of turning them into a materially viable activity**. This does not mean that everything has to be monetised, but that you can explore **what could become a stable source of income that is aligned** with who you are.

Recognising what you can get paid to do means **coming back to the concrete, to exchange, to perceived value**, without betraying your deep drive. This is where realism and intuition must work together.

What you can monetise is not always what you love most

It is often the case that what you are passionate about is not immediately monetisable — or that it becomes so over time, with adaptation. Conversely, you can be paid for things that you like **moderately**, but that you do very well.

The challenge is to **find the points of intersection**: between pleasure, skill, and real demand. Sometimes you have to know **how to transform a skill into a service or solution** that meets an existing need.

How to identify what you could offer professionally

Here are some concrete ideas:

- **Make a list of your transferable skills**: organisation, communication, writing, coaching, repair, facilitation, etc.
- **Write down the things you have already been paid or offered an exchange for** (even if it was informal).
- **Observe the market around you**: which professions, activities or formats use talents similar to yours?
- **Be open to hybrid forms**: workshops, micro-businesses, one-off services, coaching, selling content or products, etc.

Find the right balance: earn a living without losing yourself

It's not about "monetising" your passion at all costs. It's about **finding a way to support yourself financially** without exhausting yourself or betraying what matters to you.

Sometimes that means:

- Having a "bread and butter" job that leaves time for a more personal project
- Starting a side business before making it your full-time job
- Accepting a transition, a period of uncertainty or training

The important thing is to stay connected to **your inner compass**, even when navigating external constraints.

Exploration exercise

In your notebook, answer these questions:

1. What skills, services or expertise have I already been paid for or asked to provide?
2. If I had to create a paid offer tomorrow, based on what I know how to do, it would be...
3. What would be the first three concrete steps to test this idea?

By clarifying this aspect, you give **your Ikigai a concrete foundation** without sacrificing its sincerity.

SHEET 15 – Identifying your core values

You may have talent, drive, skills and even opportunities... but if what you do **conflicts with your core values**, sooner or later you will end up feeling uncomfortable, blocked or drained of energy.

Core values are like the invisible roots of your Ikigai. They determine **what is truly important to you**, what gives meaning to your actions, what allows you to feel at peace with yourself. If your choices are aligned with your values, you move forward with strength. If not, you exhaust yourself without understanding why.

What is a value?

A value is not a moral quality or a beautiful abstract idea. It is **a principle of life that guides your decisions**, consciously or unconsciously. Values are often stable over time, but can evolve with your experiences.

Examples include freedom, loyalty, creativity, autonomy, simplicity, justice, beauty, transmission, security, evolution, gentleness, commitment, and more.

You may have many, but some are **non-negotiable**: if they are violated, you immediately feel discomfort, sadness, or even anger.

How can you identify them?

Your values emerge:

- When you are deeply affected by a situation or behaviour (positively or negatively)
- When you feel proud of yourself or others
- When you feel tension or misalignment in a relationship, job, or project

In other words, **what makes you react reveals your values**.

Why knowing them is essential for your Ikigai

Your Ikigai cannot take root in the long term if you live contrary to your values. That is why it is crucial to:

- Identify them clearly
- Prioritise them (some are more important than others)
- Accept them, even if they differ from those of the people around you

This will enable you **to make better choices** that are in line with who you really are.

Practical exercise

1. **List 10 values that are important to you** from the examples above or others that come to mind.

2. **Reduce this list to 5 non-negotiable values**, those that you would be prepared to defend no matter what.
3. For each one, note a recent situation where you fully experienced it and one where it was violated.

Observe how this makes you feel. These are the values that your Ikigai should honour.

SHEET 16 – Understanding your deep needs

An authentic Ikigai is not only built on what you love or know how to do, but also on the **satisfaction of your essential needs**. Because even if you are doing the right thing, you will eventually become exhausted or feel empty if your **deep needs are not met**.

Too often, we ignore or minimise our needs because we have been taught to 'hold on', 'not rock the boat' and 'think of others before ourselves'. However, **an unmet need always comes back in the form of a lack, tension or inner fatigue**.

Understanding your needs means learning to **respect yourself deeply**.

Needs vs. desires: telling the difference

A need is not a whim or a passing fancy. It is **a vital element of your inner balance**, often universal, but whose intensity varies from person to person.

Some examples of basic needs:

- Need for security or stability
- Need for freedom, autonomy
- Need for recognition and respect
- Need for calm, solitude or silence

- Need for intensity, movement, novelty
- Need for contribution, meaning, usefulness
- Need for love, connection, belonging

Desires are often linked to objects or contexts. Needs, on the other hand, are **deep-seated, stable and non-negotiable in the long term**.

When a need is ignored...

When one of your essential needs is frustrated for too long:

- You feel restless, irritable, drained
- You have trouble concentrating or motivating yourself
- You compensate with excessive or escapist behaviour
- You feel "out of sorts" without understanding why

This is often where Ikigai becomes blurred: you try to 'do the right thing' without listening to what **you really need to feel good**.

Identify your priority needs

Take a moment to sit down and answer these questions:

1. When I'm tired or stressed, what do I miss the most?
2. At what moments in my life have I felt deeply nourished?

3. What conditions are essential for me to feel fully myself?

Observe your answers. They tell you about **your vital needs** — the ones you will need to take into account to build a lasting Ikigai.

Exercise: map your needs

Make a mind map or a simple list of your **5 most important needs today**. Then note down for each one:

- Is it being met in my current life?
- What can I do, even on a small scale, to better respect it?

This map becomes an **inner compass**. It will allow you to adjust your life choices so that you no longer betray yourself.

SHEET 17 – Identifying activities that give you energy

On the path to your Ikigai, one simple but powerful question can change everything:
"What gives me energy, rather than taking it away?"

Modern life pushes us to always do more, to tick boxes, to meet expectations. As a result, many people push **themselves to exhaustion** without really asking themselves **what recharges them**, what **nourishes them deeply**. Yet this is a fundamental benchmark: your Ikigai cannot be built **against your vitality**.

This is not about rest or recovery, but about those activities that, even when they require effort, **leave you feeling more alive, clearer, and more aligned** after experiencing them.

It's not a question of comfort, but of momentum

An activity that gives you energy may be demanding, but it **awakens something in you**. It reconnects you to a natural rhythm, puts you in a state of fluid attention, and anchors you in the present.

Conversely, some tasks may seem easy or automatic, but **leave you feeling drained, scattered, tense**.

Recognising this difference is essential to building a life that suits you.

Signs that an activity gives you energy

- You do it enthusiastically, without procrastinating
- You feel a renewed sense of clarity or calm afterwards
- You forget your fatigue while doing it
- You want to do it again, even without obligation
- You feel more confident and centred afterwards

These are not always "big things": sometimes **a simple gesture**, a human interaction or a modest creation can be enough to rekindle your inner drive.

Differentiate between energy thieves

Conversely, note what drains you:

- Certain discussions?
- Tasks that are too repetitive or disconnected from your values?
- Saying "yes" out of obligation?
- A schedule that doesn't respect your rhythm?

Identifying these things is not a judgement: it is **a valuable insight** that will help you find your way.

Practical exercise: your energy compass

In two columns, write down in your notebook:

On the left: activities or contexts that **give** me **energy**
On the right: those that **drain** my **energy**

Then ask yourself these questions:

1. Which activities in the left-hand column could I do more of during the week?
2. What can I limit or delegate in the right-hand column?
3. What small immediate changes can I make to rebalance my days?

Your Ikigai is where energy flows freely. **Learn to listen to this subtle dynamic, and it will guide you.**

SHEET 18 – Return to your childhood dreams

Before society, school or fear imposed their frameworks, **you intuitively knew what attracted you**. As a child, you were spontaneous, creative, focused on play and exploration. You knew what amused you, what fascinated you, what you did just for fun.

These impulses were not fantasies: they were **the seeds of your Ikigai**. Returning to your childhood dreams is not about escaping reality, it is **about rediscovering a forgotten truth**, a direction that you may have dismissed, but which still resonates with you today.

Childhood dreams contain valuable clues

They often speak to us:

- From your **natural imagination** (you dreamed of being an explorer, writer, vet, dancer, etc.)
- Your **way of relating to others** (more solitary or in a group, active or contemplative)
- Your **preferred language** (movement, speech, creation, care, invention, etc.)

These elements reveal what truly attracts you, **beyond external expectations**. Even if your current life is very different, you can find **the same energy** in another form.

Why these dreams have been put aside

Often, we abandon our childhood dreams because we judge them to be:

- unrealistic
- naive
- unprofitable
- "unserious"

We put them aside to do what we think we should do, to "succeed" or fit in. Yet what you loved back then **still speaks to you today**: it is an inner language to be rediscovered, not to abandon everything, but to **regain a lost sense of coherence**.

How to reintegrate them into your life

You don't have to become an astronaut or an opera singer. But you can:

- Rediscover the world of your dreams in a hobby, a project or an atmosphere
- Reconnect with the emotion associated with that dream: freedom, exploration, expression, care, play...
- Build bridges between your current activity and your deepest desires

Your Ikigai can be nourished by what your inner child has always known.

Introspective exercise: returning to the heart

In a quiet moment, ask yourself these questions and write down your answers freely:

1. When I was a child, what did I love to do, even alone, for hours on end?
2. What were my favourite games? My heroes? My imaginary friends?
3. If I could rediscover one quality from my childhood today, it would be...

Then ask yourself:
How could I honour this energy in my life today?

Even a symbolic gesture can **rekindle the flame**.

SHEET 19 – Freeing yourself from social conditioning

To live an authentic Ikigai, it is essential **to hear your own voice**, not the one the world has taught you to follow. From childhood, you have been exposed to injunctions: what to do, what is serious, what is successful, what is acceptable. Little by little, these ideas become ingrained in your mind as obvious truths... **until you forget who you are.**

This sheet invites you to **sort through what belongs to you and what you have inherited**, without judgement or rejection, but with clarity. Because you cannot build a living Ikigai on foundations that are not your own.

The traces of conditioning

These often manifest themselves in automatic thoughts:

- "That's not a real job."
- "I have to be productive to be worthy."
- "I can't disappoint"
- "You have to choose between passion and security"
- "I'm not good enough..."

These statements are not reality. They are **rules you have learned, sometimes a long time ago**, and which guide your decisions... even without you realising it.

How can you spot them?

Ask yourself this question:
If no one was watching me, if I didn't have anything to prove, what would I really do?

Often, conditioning prevents you from:

- allow yourself to explore
- changing direction
- slowing down
- choosing priorities that are not "profitable"
- daring to take a different path

Identifying these obstacles is already **a step towards regaining your decision-making power.**

Deconditioning does not mean rejecting

It's not about rejecting everything outright. Your parents, society and teachers have undoubtedly passed on **useful things too**. But today, you have the right to choose what you keep and what you leave behind.

This is a form of inner maturity: **embracing what suits you, rather than following out of habit or loyalty.**

Clarification exercise

In your notebook, divide a page into two columns:

Column 1: What I believe I "should" do in my life
Column 2: What I would really like to do (even if it is not "reasonable")

Compare the two. Which ideas are truly yours? Which ones have been passed down to you? What can you change, at your own pace, to get back to what is essential to you?

A phrase to move forward

"I choose to no longer live according to a script that is not my own."
Repeat it aloud, softly. Let it resonate.
You have just taken a key step towards your Ikigai.

SHEET 20 – Taking stock of your inner compass

You have now explored your passions, your skills, your values, your needs, your dreams, your conditioning... It is time to bring it all together. Because living your Ikigai is not just about accumulating insights, it is also **about finding a clear inner direction**, a compass that guides you in your choices, your actions and your adjustments.

This worksheet helps you **connect the scattered pieces** to bring out a more unified vision of yourself. It's not yet about "finding" your final Ikigai, but about laying the foundations for a path you can walk with confidence.

What is an inner compass?

It is a **set of personal reference points**: what sets you in motion, what stabilises you, what you reject, what nourishes you. It is not a fixed map or a rigid plan, but **a living orientation** that is unique to you.

Your inner compass does not tell you what to do at every moment, but it helps you to:

- Make decisions that are in line with who you are
- Say no without feeling guilty
- Feel when you are on the right track
- Get through periods of doubt with greater clarity

What you can include

Here are the essential elements to include in your inner compass:

1. **What makes me tick**
2. **What I do naturally well**
3. **What I want to bring to the world**
4. **What I can transform into a viable contribution**
5. **My 5 core values**
6. **My essential needs to be respected**
7. **My areas of energy, my natural impulses**
8. **Influences to unlearn or let go of**

These benchmarks are not set in stone. You can refine and add to them. But they already form a **valuable basis for moving forward.**

Exercise: your compass card

In your notebook, devote a double page to summarising

- What I have learned about myself through these last 10 sheets
- What seems most important to me to honour today
- A sentence that could summarise my current direction

Example:
"I want to live more simply, nurturing my creativity, helping others to clarify their path, without betraying myself."

This sentence does not need to be perfect. But it can become your **temporary mantra**, your guiding principle for the future.

Part 3 - Building your Ikigai step by step

SHEET 21 – Cross-referencing the 4 areas of the Ikigai diagram

You have explored the different facets of your identity in depth: what you love, what you know how to do, what you can contribute, what makes you tick. Now it's time to **connect these elements together**. It is at this stage that Ikigai takes shape, no longer as an abstract idea, but as a **living centre of alignment**.

The famous 4-circle diagram (love – know-how – be useful – be paid) becomes a concrete tool here, not to find a perfect answer, but to **detect promising areas of intersection**.

Review the four fundamental areas

1. **What you love** – your passions, your natural impulses, your sources of joy
2. **What you are good at** – your skills, talents, aptitudes
3. **What you can be paid for** – your monetisable skills, even partially
4. **What the world needs** – the concrete needs to which you can contribute

At the intersection of these areas, you begin to see **paths, forms of contribution, activities or roles that make sense**.

Create your own intersection

Take a large sheet of paper or open a new page in your notebook. Draw four circles that overlap in the centre, as in the Ikigai model.

In each circle, write down:

- 5 things you deeply love
- 5 things you are good at
- 5 areas in which you could be paid
- 5 causes, needs or topics that are important to you

Do not try to connect everything immediately. **Let this information exist together**, without forcing it to overlap.

Observe the natural connections

Once you've filled in the circles, ask yourself these questions:

- Are there any words or ideas that appear in more than one area?
- Can a passion meet a need in the world?
- Can a skill be monetised while still inspiring you?
- Does an activity bring together three out of four areas?

Note the **richest areas of intersection**, even if they are not yet clear or easy to implement. These are **your first seeds of coherence**.

Exercise: draw a first draft

In light of this exploration, write down one or two **Ikigai hypotheses**, even if they are provisional:

Examples:
– "My Ikigai could be to accompany people through life transitions through writing."
– "My Ikigai may be to create simple objects that reconnect us with nature."
– "I feel that my Ikigai revolves around teaching, connection and creativity."

These sentences are not definitive verdicts. They are **starting points to be tested, refined and embodied**.

SHEET 22 – Create a personal map of your Ikigai

Now that you have explored the four key dimensions of Ikigai, it is time to move on to a **living, personalised synthesis**: your own Ikigai map. The aim here is not to establish a single truth, but to **develop a clear, concrete and evolving vision** based on everything you have explored.

This map is a **personal reference point**, a visual or written representation that will help you stay aligned, make consistent choices and consciously adjust your trajectory.

Why create a personal map?

Because ideas remain vague until they are formalised. By putting words to paper, constructing a clear diagram or page, you will:

- Clarify your inner direction
- Anchor your discoveries in reality
- Create a source of inspiration and refocusing
- Feel that you have **a concrete guiding thread**

Your Ikigai then becomes **something you can name, look at, revisit.**

How to structure your map?

Here is a simple but powerful method for creating your personal map:

1. A central circle: your essence or mission

A sentence that sums up what gives meaning to your life (even if it is temporary)
E.g.: "To soothe and connect through listening and writing."

2. Four branches around this circle:

- What I like: 3 to 5 elements
- What I know how to do: 3 to 5 talents
- What I can bring to the world: 3 to 5 ideas
- What I can be paid for: 3 to 5 concrete ideas

You can write, draw, sketch... The main thing is that **it speaks to you, stimulates you, enlightens you**.

Minimalist version

If you prefer, you can simply fill in these sentences:

1. What makes me feel alive is...
2. What I naturally bring to the table is...
3. What I want to nurture and share is...
4. What I would like to devote more time to is...
5. My Ikigai today could be summed up as...

Consolidation exercise

Once you have finished your card:

- Read it aloud
- Close your eyes: does it resonate? Does it set you in motion, even gently?
- Leave this map open and accessible. Come back to it in a week. See what has changed, what has become clearer.

Remember: your Ikigai map is not a contract, it is **a living compass** that you can refine at any time.

SHEET 23 – Pruning parasitic projects

On the path to your Ikigai, it's not all about adding. Sometimes, it's also, and above all, about **removing**. Making room. Because if you're scattered, committed in too many directions, or held back by projects that no longer suit you, you risk **missing out on what's essential**.

Pruning is not giving up. It is **choosing with clarity**, to focus your energy on what truly makes you feel alive, useful, and aligned. It is an act of clarity and courage.

Why we hold on to projects that weigh us down

It is common to cling to projects because of:

- Fear of disappointing others
- Attachment to our self-image
- Feelings of guilt ("I have to finish what I started")
- Fear of emptiness
- A wounded ego ("I don't want to admit that this project is a failure")

But in truth, **every parasitic project is costly**: in time, mental energy, clarity. And as long as you don't let go of them, you can't welcome what truly calls to you.

How can you recognise a parasitic project?

Ask yourself these questions:

- Does this project still nourish me?
- Am I pursuing it out of enthusiasm or obligation?
- Is it distracting me from what I really want to build?
- Am I clinging to it out of fear rather than desire?

If the answers are vague, uncomfortable or tinged with heaviness, it may be time to **re-evaluate your commitment**.

Three ways to prune intelligently

1. **Consciously closing the door**
   Acknowledge that it's over, be grateful for what it has brought you, and turn the page with gratitude.
2. **Postpone with clarity**
   Decide to put this project on hold for a defined period of time to free up mental space now.
3. **Simplify**
   Transform the project into a simpler, more realistic, more flexible version.

The goal is not to "give up everything," but to **regain control** over what you choose to take on.

Project sorting exercise

Make a list of all your current projects (professional, personal, family, creative, etc.). For each one, classify it according to three columns:

1. This project deeply aligns with me
2. This project weighs me down or distracts me
3. This project needs to be transformed or simplified

Then take the first concrete action in column 2 or 3: send an email, make a decision, cancel or reschedule an appointment.

You have just freed up space for your true Ikigai.

SHEET 24 – The art of choosing a direction

On the path to your Ikigai, there comes a time when it is no longer enough to reflect, clarify or explore. You have to **choose**. A direction. A course. A first concrete step. And this choice does not need to be final: it simply needs to be **experienced**.

Many people get stuck at this stage, paralysed by the fear of making a mistake. But Ikigai is not a straight line: it is a **path that is built as you walk**. Choosing a direction does not mean giving up everything else, it means **giving your energy a point of convergence**.

The myth of the perfect choice

We often expect the right choice to be obvious, without doubt or inner conflict. But in reality:

- No choice offers any guarantees
- All paths involve a degree of uncertainty
- Commitment often comes **after** the first step, not before

You can spend years weighing up the options without ever feeling "ready". At some point, you have to **dare to try, test and experiment**, even if everything is not yet clear.

The criteria for a good choice

Rather than looking for the perfect choice, ask yourself these questions:

- Does this direction give me momentum, even if mixed with apprehension?
- Does it respect my values, my needs, my limits?
- Would it allow me to grow, learn and contribute?

If an option answers **yes** to these three questions (even partially), it is probably **the right one for you today**.

Choices are not just thought out, they are felt

Close your eyes and visualise each possible option. Feel your body. Does it tense up? Does it relax? Does your breathing become blocked or open up?

Your body often knows before your mind does. The art of choosing is also about learning to listen to that intelligence.

Exercise: set an initial course

1. Write down the two or three directions that currently appeal to you
2. For each one, write down what it would bring you... and what it would require of you
3. Choose the one that **appeals to you most today**, not for life, but for the next 3 to 6 months

4. Write this sentence:
   "I choose to move in this direction, without waiting to have all the answers."

Then take **concrete action within 48 hours**. Even if it's tiny. This is how Ikigai is activated.

SHEET 25 – Ikigai evolves over time: accept it

A common misconception is to believe that Ikigai is a stable, definitive truth, a course set once and for all. As if you had to "find" your purpose once and for all, then stick to it for the rest of your life.

In reality, **Ikigai is alive**. It transforms. It breathes with you. It changes with your experiences, your desires, and the seasons of your life. Trying to freeze it in place is a recipe for frustration. Accepting it as an evolving force allows it to **remain true and nourishing** throughout your life.

Why Ikigai changes

Here are some natural factors of change:

- Age and changing priorities
- Experiences that transform you internally
- New needs that emerge (security, freedom, calm, etc.)
- Challenges that redefine your priorities
- The discovery of new passions, talents or causes

An Ikigai that doesn't change... is often an Ikigai that **hasn't been updated**. And therefore, no longer truly reflects who you are.

Accept change without guilt

Changing direction, slowing down, closing a chapter is not betraying your path. It is **continuing it in a different way**.

But it requires courage:

- Regularly reconnect with yourself
- Re-evaluate certain choices
- Saying no to what no longer aligns with you
- Embrace the discomfort of temporary emptiness

This is not instability: it is **fidelity to your inner evolution.**

A re-adjustable compass

Think of your Ikigai as a **compass, not a GPS**. It gives you a general direction, but you are free to take detours, turn back, or stop.

And above all: **you have the right to change.** To no longer like what you used to like. To want something else. To no longer recognise yourself in what defined you yesterday.

Exercise: updating your Ikigai

In your notebook, write down:

1. What I thought was my Ikigai 5 or 10 years ago
2. What has changed in me since then

3. What feels right to me today, even if it's vague or new
4. One thing I want to explore based on this new momentum

Do this exercise regularly, for example every 6 months. You will see that your Ikigai becomes **a living thread**, not a fixed label.

SHEET 26 – How to test your Ikigai in reality

At some point, it is no longer enough to think, dream, or write in a notebook. For your Ikigai to come to life, you must **confront it with reality**, even timidly, even imperfectly. Because it is only by taking action that you will know if what you have imagined really suits you.

Testing your Ikigai does not mean giving up everything overnight or taking a big, risky leap. It means **experimenting on a small scale** to see if the momentum you feel can withstand contact with reality.

Why testing is essential

Many people idealise a new path without ever testing it. The result:

- They put it off indefinitely
- They doubt themselves more and more
- Or worse: they jump in too quickly... and crash and burn

Testing means **securing your progress** by moving forward in small steps, with intelligence, flexibility and curiosity.

Test without changing everything

Here are a few ways to test a direction without disrupting your current life:

- **Do volunteer work** in a field that appeals to you
- **Offer an initial service** for free or at a nominal fee
- **Create a blog, workshop, podcast or prototype**
- **Set aside a day or weekend to focus** on this activity
- **Meet people who are already following this path** and listen to them without judgement

The goal is not to succeed, but **to feel**: how your body reacts, what it awakens in you, what makes you want to continue.

Be attentive to feedback

After each test, ask yourself these questions:

1. Did I feel alive, aligned, useful?
2. Did I lose energy or gain clarity?
3. Do I want to explore this further, or adjust it?

The test is not there to validate once and for all, but to **help you refine your approach.**

Exercise: choose a simple test this week

1. Choose an idea, a hypothesis, an intuition related to your Ikigai

2. Decide on a simple **field test** that can be carried out within 7 days
3. Write it down in your notebook, plan it, do it
4. Then describe how you felt: tired? energised? eager to do it again?

An Ikigai does not stay in notebooks: **it lives in your actions, your attempts, your encounters.**

SHEET 27 – Adjust based on feedback

Testing a path related to your Ikigai is an essential step. But what really moves you forward is **your ability to listen to feedback, adjust and adapt**. Because even if a direction excites you at first, only experience will tell you if it truly suits you, and in what form.

Your Ikigai **is not revealed all at once**. It takes shape **through iteration**: the back-and-forth between action, feeling, reflection, and reorientation. It is a living, flexible process that requires listening to signals — both internal and external.

Feedback is information, not a verdict

It is easy to become discouraged if a test does not yield the expected results. However, every piece of feedback, every feeling, every reaction from others is **valuable data** that allows you to adjust your course.

Here are some examples of feedback to look out for:

- Your **energy level** after taking action
- The **pleasure or discomfort** felt during the activity
- **External feedback** (even subtle): encouragement, silence, questions
- Your own **spontaneous thoughts**: do you want to do it again? Run away? Refine it?

The goal is not to succeed at everything, but to **better understand what really suits you.**

Knowing how to pivot without questioning everything

Adjusting does not mean giving up. Sometimes it means:

- Changing the format (switching from a blog to a video, from a workshop to individual coaching)
- Adapting your pace (slowing down, structuring, simplifying)
- Reducing the scale (starting smaller to rediscover enjoyment)
- Shifting the framework (changing your audience, location, or approach)

Your Ikigai does not necessarily change. It is simply that **the way you express it** becomes clearer.

Exercise: reviewing a test

In your notebook, choose an action you have recently tried and answer these questions:

1. What worked well?
2. What exhausted or frustrated me?
3. What would I do differently next time?
4. What does this tell me about myself, my rhythm, my Ikigai?

Finish with this sentence:
"I choose to readjust without judging myself. My Ikigai is becoming clearer step by step."

SHEET 28 – Taking small, concrete steps

On the path to Ikigai, the temptation to make a "big change" can be strong. We dream of leaving everything behind, starting over, transforming everything at once. But in reality, it is often **the sum of small, consistent steps** that leads to a life in alignment.

A small step is not an insignificant step. It is a **symbolic**, **repeated act** that brings you closer to your truth. It does not require you to know everything, to be ready, or to take a leap into the unknown. It just requires you to start where you are, **with what you have.**

Why small steps are powerful

- They reduce fear: you don't have to risk everything
- They build confidence: each step feeds momentum
- They produce visible results: what seemed vague becomes tangible
- They build momentum: what was "far away" becomes "in progress"

Small steps are **the antidote to mental paralysis**. They turn intention into reality.

Concrete examples

If your Ikigai revolves around writing:
→ write for 10 minutes every morning, publish a post, join a workshop

If you want to support others:
→ listen attentively to a loved one, offer a trial session, read a book on active listening

If you dream of a creative or community project:
→ set aside a fixed time slot each week to think about it, talk to someone you trust, create a first draft

The right small step is one that is **simple enough to do today**, but **engaging enough to create momentum.**

The trap: waiting until you are ready

You will never have all the guarantees. The timing will never be perfect.
The best time to take a small step towards your Ikigai **is now.**

You can spend your life thinking about it... or choose to test yourself, one step at a time, with kindness.

Exercise: your step for the week

Take a minute to write down the answer to this question: **What small step can I take this week to nurture my Ikigai?**

Then write down:

- When you are going to do it
- How long it will take
- How you will feel afterwards

Then... do it. And observe how it changes you.

SHEET 29 – Ikigai is not a job but a way of being

One of the biggest misconceptions about Ikigai is to believe that it is a **job to be found**, an ideal position, a perfect career where everything is aligned. This reductive view can become a prison: until you have "found the right job", you believe that you are not yet in the right place.

But your Ikigai **is not a social function**, it is not a status to display on LinkedIn. It is a **quality of presence to yourself and the world**, which can be embodied in any role, context or activity. It does not depend on your business card, but on **how you live each moment**.

A common mistake: reducing Ikigai to work

Of course, work can be a powerful expression of Ikigai. But it does not sum it up. Many people find their Ikigai:

- in the way they raise a child
- in the care they take in cultivating a garden
- in their way of listening, communicating, and creating bonds
- in a neighbourhood project, a discreet art, an invisible commitment

Seeking Ikigai **solely through a profession** risks **overlooking what already has meaning, here and now.**

What "way of being" means

Your Ikigai is revealed:

- in your **perspective** on what you do
- in **the intention** you put into every action
- in the **consistency** between your values, your actions and your words
- in **the quality of** your **presence**, more than in your performance

This is what makes some people shine even in a modest job, and others seem dull despite a brilliant career.

How to live your Ikigai without changing jobs

- By bringing meaning to your interactions
- By creating a space for personal expression in your daily life
- By ritualising what connects you to yourself (walking, writing, meditation, etc.)
- By changing **your inner attitude** towards external constraints

Your Ikigai is not what you do, it is **what you embody when you do it.**

Exercise: embody your Ikigai today

In your notebook, write:

1. One thing you do regularly that you could **find more meaning** in
2. A quality you would like **to embody more consciously** in your daily life (e.g. listening, calmness, clarity, generosity...)

Then choose **a specific moment in your day** to practise this quality... whatever the task.

You have just activated your Ikigai in the present moment.

SHEET 30 – Living your Ikigai even in a "bread and butter" job

You may be in a situation where your current job **does not inspire you**, but you cannot leave it right away. It is secure, it pays the bills, it leaves you little room for manoeuvre.
So, do you have to wait until you leave it to start living your Ikigai?
No. Because **your Ikigai does not depend on a radical change**. It can begin to express itself **even in a bread-and-butter job**, provided you change your perspective on it... and how you use it.

Don't confuse constraint with imprisonment

Just because you have a job you're not passionate about doesn't mean your life is meaningless. Even if it's not perfect, this job can be:

- A source of stability from which to build something else on the side
- A place for observation, learning and service
- A space where you can exercise certain **qualities** that bring you closer to yourself

The important thing is not to identify yourself solely with this role. You are **much more than your job.**

3 ways to live your Ikigai despite everything

1. Find meaning in the little things
Even in a repetitive job, you can cultivate rigour, kindness, listening skills, clarity... These are valuable expressions of your Ikigai.

2. Develop your Ikigai in parallel
Set aside time—even if it's just a little—each week for what makes you tick. An activity, research, a project, a practice... Feed your passion outside of working hours.

3. Use your job as a springboard, not an excuse
Your current job can help you **finance**, **prepare for**, or **structure** your transition to a more aligned lifestyle. But this requires a clear intention, even if it's discreet at first.

It's not the job that extinguishes your passion... it's forgetting yourself

The real trap is not doing a job to "pay the bills", it's believing that it defines your worth or prevents you from being yourself.
Your Ikigai **feeds on your attention**, not your job. It begins to exist **as soon as you recognise it and choose to honour it, even a little.**

Exercise: change your attitude

In your notebook, answer these questions:

1. In my current job, is there a quality that I can consciously cultivate?

2. Outside of this job, what regular action can I take to nurture my Ikigai?
3. What long-term vision would give meaning to this period?

Write down a **commitment statement**, such as: **"I choose to use my job as a foundation, not as a cage."**

Part 4: Ritualising Ikigai in everyday life

SHEET 31 – Create an aligned morning routine

How you start your day often determines the quality of everything that follows. Before you even open your emails, get in the car or respond to your obligations, you have an opportunity: **to perform a simple, symbolic gesture that connects you to your Ikigai.**

Creating an **aligned morning routine** is not about piling on productive tasks, but carefully choosing **what grounds you, uplifts you, and refocuses you.** Even ten minutes is enough, if you live them mindfully.

Why the morning is a key moment

When you wake up, your mind is still fresh, open and uncluttered. It's the ideal time to:

- Come back to yourself before turning to the world
- Anchoring an intention
- Create a link between your inner self and your future actions
- Defining a rhythm that is right for you

An aligned routine **nourishes your Ikigai from the very first minutes of the day.**

What an aligned routine can contain

There is no single recipe. Your routine should **reflect who you are**, be realistic and flexible, but also meaningful. Here are a few possible elements:

- A few conscious breaths or stretches
- An inspiring read, a few lines from a journal
- Write down an intention, a keyword, or a guiding phrase for the day
- Return to your Ikigai card or a quality you wish to embody
- Meditate, walk, drink herbal tea in silence...
- Visualise a small step to take during the day

Even 5 to 10 minutes can make all the difference.

The trap to avoid: being too demanding

An aligned routine is not a new challenge to be conquered. It is not a spiritual to-do list. It's okay if you skip a day. What matters is **gentle regularity**, a natural return to this ritual when you feel scattered.

The goal is not perfection, but **faithfulness to yourself**.

Exercise: create your own personal ritual

In your notebook, complete the following sentences:

1. In the morning, I need to...

2. What reconnects me to myself is...
3. I could devote ___ minutes each morning to...
4. My intention for this week:

Then try out your routine for 7 days. Adjust it according to how you feel. You have just laid **the daily foundation** for embodying your Ikigai.

SHEET 32 – Nourishing your vital energy

You may have a clear vision of your Ikigai, a notebook filled with intentions, a beautiful roadmap... but if your **vital energy is low**, you will not be able to embody what drives you.

Ikigai is not just about meaning: it's also about **vitality**, energy and inner balance. That's why nourishing your energy is **a fundamental pillar** of your aligned daily life.

What exactly is vital energy?

It is that **inner strength that allows you to act, create, love, decide and persevere.**

It is not constant, but is **influenced by your lifestyle choices**: diet, sleep, movement, thoughts, relationships, environment...

When your vital energy is nourished:

- You feel clear, stable, alive
- You bounce back more easily
- You enjoy taking action
- Your emotions are more balanced

Ikigai does not require great strength, but it does require **a minimum level of stable and sustained energy.**

Things that drain your energy (without you realising it)

- Too many digital demands
- Too much mental distraction
- Unbalanced relationships
- A disorganised diet
- Lack of exercise or deep rest
- Acting against your needs or values

Every energy drain takes you further away from your inner core. Conversely, every act of self-care brings you back to it.

The 4 pillars to nourish it

1. **Breathe consciously** – even for just 3 minutes a day
2. **Move regularly** and gently: walk, stretch, dance
3. **Rest truly**, with moments of deep disconnection
4. **Connect with living things**: nature, silence, reading, sincere human contact

It's not about revolutionising everything, but about **honouring your energy as a sacred resource.**

Exercise: your mini energy plan

In your notebook, write:

1. What drains my energy the most right now:

2. One simple thing I could stop or reduce:
3. One simple thing I could start or strengthen:
4. A specific time during the week when I will take care of my energy:

Then note at the end of the week: **What has changed in me?**

SHEET 33 – Taking care of your body and mind

Ikigai is not a spiritual abstraction. It is embodied **in a living body, filled with emotions, impulses and limitations.** Taking care of your Ikigai therefore also means **taking care of yourself** as a whole: body, mind and heart.

Without a minimum of mental clarity, physical presence and emotional balance, it becomes difficult to feel what is right, to make aligned choices, or to act with consistency. Your **inner ecosystem** is the breeding ground for your Ikigai.

The body is the messenger of your alignment

You probably already know this, but it's important to remember: **your body speaks to you.**
It tells you when you are in the right place (feeling of openness, lightness) and when you are not (tension, unexplained fatigue, knot in your stomach).

The more connected you are to your body, the more you will:

- Make decisions that are in line with who you are
- Feel when it's time to say no, slow down or pivot
- Seize opportunities when they arise

Listening to your body is like listening to your living compass.

The mind, too, needs hygiene

Your thoughts can support your Ikigai... or distract you from it. If you live in a constant stream of critical or anxious thoughts, it becomes difficult to hear your deepest impulses.

Taking care of your mind means:

- Calming the mind with rituals (breathing, writing, silence)
- Questioning automatic thoughts ("I'm not ready", "I'm not good enough...")
- Choosing what you feed: content, relationships, environments

A clear mind **leaves room for your Ikigai to express itself.**

In practice: simple steps to achieve balance

- A **hot drink** in the morning, with full attention
- **3 minutes of conscious breathing** before making a decision
- A quick **body scan** (where are the tensions today?)
- **One self-care action per day** (massage, rest, water, stretching, etc.)
- A moment to **organise your thoughts** in a notebook or during a walk

These are **modest but powerful daily actions.**

Exercise: gentle diagnosis

In your notebook, write down:

1. What am I already doing to take care of my body?
2. What am I doing for my mind?
3. Which area (body or mind) needs more attention this week?
4. What small, concrete steps will I take in this direction?

Your body and mind are not tools: they are your **deepest allies.** Take care of them, and your Ikigai will take root.

SHEET 34 – Surround yourself with nourishing relationships

No one experiences their Ikigai alone. Even if your path is a personal one, it is **supported, slowed down or energised** by the quality of the relationships around you.
Some relationships lift you up, refocus you, and inspire you.
Others distract you, devalue you, or drain you.
Learning to **consciously choose your relationships** is one of the most powerful ways to anchor your Ikigai in reality.

The invisible impact of those around you

Every day, without realising it, you absorb the energy of the people around you:

The way they speak

Their beliefs, fears, and projections

Their pace, their stress, their confidence (or lack thereof)

If you are surrounded by people who doubt everything, criticise, complain or do not believe in you... it becomes difficult to stay on course.
Conversely, a single kind glance, a well-chosen word, a discreet but steady presence can **rekindle your inner fire.**

What is a nurturing relationship?

It is not necessarily a "perfect" or symbiotic relationship. It is a relationship that, **over time**, allows you to:

Be fully yourself

Dare to express what is important to you

Feel respected, listened to, supported

Progress together, even in silence

Nurturing relationships do not require effort to exist. **They breathe naturally.**

How to sort things out without violence

There's no need to abruptly cut all ties that weigh you down. But you can:

Consciously create distance from certain people (less time, less expectation)

Strengthen what is alive in your healthy relationships

Choose who to share your Ikigai projects with, to protect them from premature criticism

Seek out new circles: courses, workshops, spaces for expression, supportive communities

Your relational environment is an **ecosystem**. It can lift you up or drag you down.

Exercise: your support circle

In your notebook, draw two circles:

In the inner circle, write down 3 to 5 people who **nourish, inspire or support** you

In the outer circle, write down those who **drain, slow down or misalign** you

Then ask yourself this question:
How can I nurture the first circle... and set healthy boundaries with the second?

Your Ikigai grows best **in a peaceful and lively relational climate.**

SHEET 35 – Finding meaning in the little things

We often believe that the meaning of life lies in big decisions, major upheavals and significant commitments. But Ikigai, in its original Japanese wisdom, is not just about great achievements. It slips **quietly** into the simplest of actions: making tea, tidying up a space, walking, saying hello, really listening.

Finding meaning in the little things means stopping believing that you have to do more to exist. It means choosing to **be mindful of what you already experience.** It means cultivating a way of life that transforms the mundane into the sacred.

The ordinary is sacred ground

Every moment of the day can become **a meeting point with yourself**:

Washing the dishes while listening to your breathing

Preparing a meal in silence, with care

Saying thank you with attention

Putting something away with respect

Look at a tree, a light, a face... and feel life

It's not what you do that gives meaning, **it's how you do it.**

Why this changes everything

When you find meaning in the ordinary:

You feel less empty, less scattered

Your daily life becomes a source of Ikigai, even without "big plans"

You reconnect with the beauty of the present

You rediscover the power to create meaning, here and now

The quality of your attention transforms the quality of your life.

How to cultivate this attention

Deliberately slow down for a few minutes each day

Do one thing at a time, with presence

Choose a mundane action (drinking a cup of tea, opening a window...) and ritualise it

Ask yourself the question: "What am I experiencing right now?"

Say a word with intention (hello, thank you, I'm listening)

These micro-actions **realign your perspective with what really matters.**

Exercise: the ritual of the day

Every evening, in your notebook or in your mind, answer this question:

"What small moment gave me meaning today?"

It doesn't have to be an exceptional event. Look for the **subtle things**. Little by little, you will learn to recognise that your Ikigai is not built tomorrow... but **already, here.**

SHEET 36 – Learning to slow down to feel better

We live in a world that values speed, efficiency and productivity. However, Ikigai does not reveal itself in haste. It **needs silence, space and slowness** to emerge. Learning to slow down is not a waste of time. It is **a way of reconnecting with yourself**, your body, your impulses and your deepest truths. It is about creating a rhythm of life that allows you to **feel**, rather than simply react.

Why slowing down changes the quality of your life

When you slow down:

Your thoughts calm down, your mind clears

Your emotions become clearer

Your body becomes your guide again

You can discern what nourishes you... and what tires you

You reconnect with your true needs and desires

Deep feelings only emerge in calmness. Noise distances you from them.

Slowing down does not mean stopping everything

It is not about shirking your responsibilities or living in slow motion. It is about **creating pockets of calm** in your day. Bubbles of slowness to **savour what you are experiencing**, and no longer rush through life like a breathless runner.

This could be:

A 10-minute screen-free break

A slow, mindful walk

A shower experienced as meditation

A meal without multitasking

Choosing to breathe before responding

The link between slowness and Ikigai

Your Ikigai is not loud. It is found in the tiny, the subtle, the inner echo.
If you are constantly busy, agitated, in a hurry, you will not hear it.

By slowing down, you open a door to it. You begin to perceive what touches you, animates you, makes you feel alive... without forcing it.

Exercise: a day with deliberate slowdowns

Identify three moments in your day when you will **intentionally slow down** (e.g., morning, mealtimes, late afternoon).

At each of these times, choose to **do less, but with more presence.**

At the end of the day, write down how you felt and what you perceived more clearly.

You have just created windows to feel what wants to live within you.

SHEET 37 – Being of service without forgetting yourself

Ikigai, in its deepest sense, often involves **some form of contribution**. You feel that you have something to offer: knowledge, talent, listening skills, presence, energy.
But offering does not mean exhausting yourself. Being of service does not mean **sacrificing yourself**.
Finding your Ikigai also means **finding the right balance** between giving of yourself and respecting yourself.

The impulse to contribute: a natural driving force

When you are connected to what truly drives you, you **want to share it.** Not to be recognised, but because it overflows. Because it makes sense. Because it connects you.

In this context, being of service means:

Giving with joy, not out of duty

Feeling nourished at the same time as giving

Acting without expecting immediate return

Touching something greater than yourself

It is a living service, not an imposed role.

When service becomes self-forgetfulness

Many generous people forget themselves. They give... until they burn out. They say yes... without listening to themselves. They carry everything... and end up exhausted.

Signs that you are forgetting yourself:

Chronic fatigue, irritability, feelings of injustice

Loss of pleasure in what you used to enjoy giving

Difficulty setting boundaries

Need to be useful in order to exist

Authentic service **does not drain you. It connects you.**

Finding the right balance

A few simple guidelines:

Before saying yes, ask yourself: "Is this right for me here and now?"

Learn to say no **without guilt**, so you can say yes to what really matters

Offer what you can **without forcing yourself or betraying yourself**

Take care of your energy **as much as that of others**

Being of service also means **inspiring others by staying centred.**

Exercise: your inner compass

In your notebook, answer these two sets of questions

Where do I serve with joy?
→ What does it bring me? What do I radiate in those moments?

Where do I serve others while forgetting myself?
→ What can I adjust, put in place, or delegate to regain balance?

Add a reminder sentence:
"I can contribute without sacrificing myself. My Ikigai includes me."

SHEET 38 – Ikigai Journal: a tool for alignment

The outside world is constantly changing, your emotions fluctuate, your desires evolve... In this constant movement, it is easy to lose your way.
To stay connected to your Ikigai, nothing beats a **stable, intimate and free space**: your journal.

A simple notebook, kept with sincerity and consistency, can become **a powerful tool for clarity, grounding and realignment.** It allows you to take stock, follow your impulses, readjust your choices, and above all... listen to what lives within you.

Why a journal is so powerful

Writing is not just "jotting down your thoughts". It is:

Giving shape to what is vague

Getting out of your head and into your heart

Observing your progress over time

Taking a step back from what you are experiencing

Feeling what is aligned... or not

It is a **benevolent mirror**, a space of gentle truth, without judgement.

How to use it to nurture your Ikigai

You can come back to it as often as you like, without any pressure. Here are a few simple suggestions:

Morning: set an intention ("Today, I want to live...")

Evening: note down a moment of alignment or awareness

Weekly: take stock of your actions, feelings, adjustments

Monthly: reread, highlight, extract key phrases or recurring dreams

When in doubt: write without filtering for 10 minutes... and listen to what comes up

5 powerful questions to ask yourself regularly

What gave me energy this week?

What weighed me down or drained me?

Do I feel aligned with my current choices?

What have I avoided doing or looking at? Why?

What small adjustment could bring me closer to my Ikigai?

These simple questions bring you back **to your core.**

Exercise: create your writing ritual

In your notebook, define:

The time you would like to write (morning? evening?)

The frequency that suits you (daily? 3 times a week?)

The tone you want to adopt (free, spontaneous, structured?)

Then... get started. Even if it's just one sentence. You're not writing to do well. You're writing to **reconnect.**

SHEET 39 – Celebrating small successes

On the path to Ikigai, we often look too far ahead. We focus on what remains to be done, on what is missing, on what is not yet perfect. As a result, we forget to **see and honour the progress we have already made**.

Celebrating small successes means cultivating **gratitude for your own journey.** It is not pride or self-satisfaction. It is **a practice of conscious joy** that nourishes your energy, motivation and confidence.

Why it's essential

Your brain is naturally drawn to the negative (what's wrong, what's incomplete). To counterbalance this tendency, you need **to train your eye to see the positive, however subtle it may be.**

When you celebrate:

You reinforce the desire to move forward

You integrate your progress instead of minimising it

You develop healthy and stable self-esteem

You anchor habits that are aligned with your Ikigai

Every small victory is a milestone on your journey.

What kinds of successes should you celebrate?

Not just the big milestones. On the contrary:

A sincere conversation you wouldn't have had before

A respectful 'no'

A routine you've kept up for three days in a row

A moment of inner clarity

A difficult emotion gently navigated

An idea put down on paper

What matters is not the size of the step, but the intention behind it.

How can you celebrate in a practical way?

By writing it down in your journal: "Today, I managed to..."

By treating yourself to a small gesture of gratitude (a break, flowers, a walk, music...)

By sharing it with someone who cares

By speaking gently to yourself: "I am proud of what I have done."

This is an **exercise in seeing yourself with kindness.**

Exercise: the little victories notebook

Create a special page in your notebook. Title it: **"What I have achieved, even if it is small."**

And every day, write down one thing, no matter how small. Reread this page regularly. It will become **a treasure trove of concrete evidence that you are already living your Ikigai.**

SHEET 40 – Living Ikigai in difficult times

Ikigai is not just for easy days, periods of enthusiasm or moments of clarity. It takes **on its full strength and depth** when life becomes more blurred, more difficult, more unstable.

Grief, illness, loss, mental exhaustion, deep doubt... These moments can take us away from our momentum. But they are also **gateways to a more sincere, more essential version** of our Ikigai.

Do not confuse pain with misalignment.

It is natural to go through difficult times. This is not a sign of failure. It is not proof that you have made a mistake. It is a time of slowing down, of forced introspection, sometimes of stripping back.

Even during these periods, your Ikigai **continues to live within you**, often in a more discreet way:

In an act of care

In a silent presence

In the simple act of carrying on, despite everything

What should you do in these moments?

Don't force it: accept that your rhythm is changing. Rest.

Get back to basics: let go of your goals, stay connected to what matters most to you.

Listen to what remains: even in chaos, certain desires and values remain. They are your guiding thread.

Surround yourself with gentleness: people, places and actions that bring you peace.

Express what you are going through: through writing, speaking, drawing, or mindful silence.

Ikigai as an inner light

Ikigai is not a performance. It is a **living relationship with what connects you to life**, even when it is hard. In difficult times, it becomes **more humble, more profound, more intimate.**

Sometimes, it's just:

Looking at a tree

Feeling your breath

Saying "I'm still here"

Listening without running away

Crying when you feel it makes sense

Exercise: the stable core

In your notebook, answer this question:
"Even if everything around me is falling apart... what within me remains standing?"

Then write down a key phrase to reread on dark days. For example:
"I don't need to be well to remain true to what drives me."

Part 5: Passing on, evolving, shining

SHEET 41 – Becoming a model of alignment

Living your Ikigai is not only a personal benefit. It is a **natural source of inspiration** for others.
Without speeches or attempts to convince, your way of being, your choices, your energy and your priorities become a **living example of consistency**.
That is what it means to be a model of alignment: not preaching, but shining.

Alignment can be seen... and felt

Aligned people have a special presence. They are not perfect, but they:

Know why they get up in the morning

Act with meaning and clarity

Make choices in line with their values

Inspire confidence, calm, or enthusiasm simply by the way they are

You don't need to be charismatic. You just need to be **deeply yourself.**

Why this is naturally inspiring

Because it's rare. In a world where many wear masks, seek to please, or run away from their truths, a person centred on their Ikigai **offers a silent reference point.**

They show that it is possible to:

To listen to your inner voice

To make courageous choices

To live with simplicity and integrity

To navigate difficulties with meaning

You become a mirror of what is possible.

Please note: being a role model does not mean being perfect

It is not about becoming perfect or imposing yourself as a reference point. It is about:

Living your Ikigai with authenticity

Accepting your limitations and doubts

Being true to yourself, even in your imperfections

Continuing to move forward, humbly

It's not what you do that inspires, it's how you live it.

Exercise: your invisible footprint

Take a moment to answer these questions in your notebook:

When have I been touched by someone who is aligned? What did this person convey to me without saying it?

And what do I convey without knowing it? Through my choices, my words, my silences...

Which aspect of my Ikigai is most visible to others?

And what aspect would I like to embody more clearly?

You don't have anything to prove. Just **allow yourself to be aligned**... and let the rest shine through.

SHEET 42 – Ikigai in relationships and family

Ikigai is sometimes thought of as a personal, almost solitary path. In reality, **it deeply affects your relationships**, because living in alignment impacts the way you love, communicate, educate and set boundaries. Ikigai is lived out in your choices... but also in the **way you relate to others**, starting with those closest to you: partners, children, parents, friends.

When your loved ones sense that something has changed

When you start living according to your Ikigai:

You have more clarity in your priorities

You are more authentic, more present, more stable

You express your needs calmly

You no longer get lost in the expectations or opinions of others

This may come as a surprise. Sometimes it may be unsettling. But often, it **opens up new space in your relationships.**

Balancing individuality and connection

Living your Ikigai **does not mean shunning connections** or imposing your vision. It means finding:

How to be yourself, without denying who you are

How to stay connected without betraying yourself

How to inspire without forcing

How to communicate without trying to convince

Relationships become healthier when **everyone respects their place, their needs and their rhythms.**

Ikigai in the family: presence, example, transmission

You don't need grand speeches to pass on Ikigai to your children or loved ones:

Be present in what you are experiencing

Name your choices, your doubts, your impulses

Let them see what drives you

Teach them to listen to their own impulses, not to copy yours

Your life is the message.

Exercise: adjust your relationships to your Ikigai

In your notebook, choose 1 to 2 key relationships (family, partner, friendship) and answer:

Do I feel free to be myself?

Can I express what is important to me?

What can I adjust (words, pace, gestures) so that this relationship supports my Ikigai – rather than hindering it?

Often, a simple change in attitude **is enough to transform the entire relationship.**

SHEET 43 – Creating a meaningful project

Living your Ikigai can take many forms: a job, a work of art, a daily gesture, a way of being. But for many, there is a need to **materialise this inner drive in a concrete project**, something that gives meaning, connects, and impacts the world, even on a small scale.

Creating a meaningful project is **giving substance to your Ikigai**. It is not necessarily a business or a humanitarian mission. It is a space for expression that reflects who you are, recharges your batteries and connects you.

What is an aligned project?

An aligned project is born at the intersection of:

What you love to do

What you know how to do

What moves you deeply

What can be useful to others, even in a small way

It can be big or small, visible or discreet. What matters is that it **comes from within**.

Some examples of meaningful projects

Create a blog, podcast or channel on a subject that inspires you

Designing a workshop, coaching programme or training course

Write a book, set up an association, launch a local initiative

Make, sew, cook, sing... and share

Offer your time, a listening ear, or your presence where it is needed

Meaning does not come from the format, but from the intention.

The 3 keys to an Ikigai project

Clarity: What do you really want to convey or create? Why does it matter to you?

Simplicity: There's no need to aim too high right away. An aligned project can start with a very modest action.

Joy: Does it give you momentum and energy? If not, readjust.

An Ikigai project **grows with you.** It evolves, transforms and accompanies you.

Exercise: lay the foundations for your project

In your notebook, answer these questions:

If I could start a project without fear or pressure, what would I do?

What do I already have at my disposal (time, skills, desires)?

What first step could I take this week?

Often, all it takes is **one step**, and everything starts to fall into place.

SHEET 44 – Inspiring others without preaching

When you start living according to your Ikigai, it's natural to want **to share that joy, clarity and renewed energy**.
But beware of a common pitfall: wanting to convince, correct, or "awaken" others at all costs.
Ikigai is not a universal truth to be imposed, but **a personal path to embody.**

Inspiring others is not about speaking louder. It's about **living more authentically.**

The trap of unintentional proselytising

When you find a path that works for you, you may want your loved ones to follow it. But wanting to "convert" them can:

Create resistance

Generate guilt or comparison in others

Diminish the power of your own path

Silent example is often more powerful than words.

What truly inspires

The people who inspire us are rarely the ones who talk the most. They are the ones who:

Radiate inner peace

Make consistent choices

Dare to be themselves

Move forward despite doubt

Listen more than they speak

They do not impose anything. They **inspire through their presence.**

How to share without imposing

Talk about yourself, not others ("this is what makes me feel good", not "you should do the same")

Offer an example, not a model

Embrace different paces: everyone has their own timing and stages

Let others follow their own path, even if it is very different from yours

This respect opens more doors than any argument ever could.

Exercise: transform the desire to convince into an inspiring presence

In your notebook, answer these three questions:

Who has inspired me without ever giving me advice? Why?

When did I want to convince someone? What did that say about my own needs (recognition, validation, fear, etc.)?

How can I simply embody what drives me, without imposing it on others?

Your inner fire can warm without burning.

SHEET 45 – Learning to pass on your experience

When you walk the path of Ikigai, a natural step eventually presents itself: **the need to share.** Not to teach, convince or 'save', but simply to **share what we have understood, experienced and gone through**. Sharing is an act of connection. A form of giving. A way of extending your Ikigai to others.

Why share?

Because your path can enlighten someone else

Because saying things helps you to integrate them more fully

Because passing on knowledge gives new depth to your experience

Because you become **the bridge between what you have learned... and those who are still searching**

Sincere sharing **enriches both sides of the relationship**: the giver and the receiver.

What you can share

You don't need to be an "expert". You can share:

Your insights

Your failures and what they taught you

Your routines, your tools, your impulses

Your way of overcoming doubts

Your small steps, your big turns

What you have experienced with your heart is valuable.

Possible ways of passing it on

A discussion with a loved one who is searching for meaning

A post on social media, an article, a video

A workshop, a circle, a podcast

Individual coaching

A journal that you make public

Or simply... your everyday way of being

The form doesn't matter. What matters is **the right intention**.

Exercise: what you have to convey

In your journal, answer these three questions:

What have I experienced that I would have liked to hear, receive or read at the time?

Who around me could benefit from some of my experience?

What form of communication would seem simple and natural for me to try?

Then, write down a first small action: a message, a sharing, an idea.

Sharing is offering a little light... without expecting anything in return.

SHEET 46 – Listening to the calls of evolution

Even when you are living in alignment, **the path of Ikigai is never fixed.**
Your being evolves. Your needs change. Your energy transforms. What motivated you yesterday may be redefined tomorrow.
Ikigai is not a fixed goal, but **a living movement**. Learning to listen to its calls for evolution is key to staying true to yourself.

Those moments when "it no longer resonates"

Sometimes, without warning:

An activity that you were passionate about becomes burdensome

A relationship seems to be dragging you down

A project loses its meaning

Your energy drops for no apparent reason

These are not failures. They are often **signs that something within you is calling for change.**

Recognising the signs of an inner calling

These calls are sometimes subtle:

A recurring feeling of discomfort

An irrational but persistent desire

Revealing jealousy – what if it were a repressed aspiration?

Unexplained fatigue that hides a need for transformation

Your body, your emotions, your daydreams are speaking to you. **Listen to them.**

Do not confuse loyalty with rigidity

Staying true to your Ikigai does not mean **locking yourself into an image, a role, or a project.** On the contrary, it means:

Accepting that you are evolving

Sometimes questioning what you believed to be established

Letting go of certain things in order to welcome new ones

Evolution is part of the living process of Ikigai.

Exercise: detecting a call for evolution

In your notebook, answer these three questions:

What in my current life no longer seems to nourish me as it once did?

What attracts me, even timidly, but I don't yet dare to explore?

If I were to listen to this call, what small first step could I take?

Ikigai does not betray itself by changing. It **refines, deepens and adapts.**

SHEET 47 – Regularly renewing your Ikigai

Ikigai is not a fixed answer that you discover once and for all. It is **a living process** that needs to be updated, questioned and adapted as the seasons of your life change. Your desires, your strengths, your constraints and your circumstances evolve. **So does your Ikigai.**

Renewing your Ikigai means **honouring your inner dynamics** and continuing to adjust, with awareness.

Why it's normal to have to "go back to the drawing board"

You have changed

Your priorities have shifted

What motivated you before has fulfilled its purpose

A life event has shaken up your bearings

You feel it is time to start a new chapter

This is not a crisis. It is an **invitation to realign yourself.**

When and how should you do this "Ikigai assessment"?

Take the time, once or twice a year, to do a thorough review. Sit down in a quiet place with something to write with, and explore the four areas:

What I deeply love → Have I nurtured this area recently?

What I know how to do / my talents → Have I developed, used, or neglected certain skills?

What I believe the world needs → Has my awareness changed? Is there a cause that appeals to me more?

What I can be paid for → Does my current situation allow me to live with dignity while remaining aligned?

These questions **help you to re-map your current Ikigai.**

A practice to adopt: "Ikigai cycles"

At the beginning of each season, set three Ikigai intentions (pleasure/usefulness/development).

At each solstice or birthday, look back on your journey

Use your journal to note any shifts, desires, or recurring intuitions

Let a **more current Ikigai** emerge**, one that is closer to who you have become**

You don't need to change everything. Sometimes, **a simple realignment is enough.**

Exercise: create your renewal ritual

In your notebook:

Choose a symbolic date (birthday, start of the year, new moon, equinox, etc.).

Create an annual or quarterly space to ask yourself this question:
"What do I really want to nurture in my life today?"

This appointment with yourself is a **living compass**.

SHEET 48 – Creating a life with less but better

Living your Ikigai is not about doing more, accumulating more, or filling every minute with activity.
It is often the opposite: **eliminating the superfluous**, slowing down, simplifying... to leave more room for the essential.
Creating a life with less but better means choosing **quality of presence over quantity of things.**

The illusion of "always more"

The modern world values:

Productivity

Constant busyness

Visible success

Rapid consumption

But Ikigai speaks of:

Meaning

Inner joy

Authentic connection

Of subtle contribution

Less noise, more alignment.

What "less but better" can mean

Fewer obligations chosen out of fear, more choices made out of impulse

Fewer possessions, more free time

Less distraction, more depth

Fewer superficial social relationships, more genuine connections

Less agitation, more nourishing silence

This is not a reduction, it is a **clarification.**

How to start simplifying your life

Sort through your activities, possessions, habits and relationships with care

Ask yourself: "Does this truly nourish my Ikigai?"

Keep what uplifts you, enlightens you, centres you

Let go of the rest, without guilt

Celebrate the space you've gained – inside and out

Lightening your load means opening up space to breathe.

Exercise: your "less but better" list

In your notebook, draw two columns:

On the left: "I want less of..." (stress, screens, judgements, unnecessary purchases, etc.)

On the right: "I want more..." (slowness, nature, reading, authentic moments...)

Choose **one small change to implement this week.** This path towards "less but better" is **one of the surest ways to achieve lasting Ikigai.**

SHEET 49 – When doubt returns: what to do?

Even with a clear Ikigai, even after years of alignment, **doubt can return.**
One day, a question arises: "What if I was wrong?", "Is this still the right path?", "Why don't I feel that clarity anymore?"

These periods are natural. They do not necessarily call your Ikigai into question.
They invite you to **dig deeper**, to listen differently.

What doubt reveals

Doubt is often:

A sign of inner transition

A need to slow down and readjust

A call for more truth

A phase of maturation between two stages

It **does not mean that you have failed.** It means that you are alive and evolving.

What should you do in these moments?

Do not run away from doubt. Embrace it. Write down your questions.

Slow down your actions. Let the silence speak to you.

Reread your diary, your old impulses, your past choices.

Go back to basics: what makes you feel good?

Talk to someone you trust. Being listened to helps to clarify things.

Doubt is not a break, it is often a transformation.

Do not confuse doubt with a loss of meaning.

You may have doubts about a project, a form, or a stage. That doesn't mean your Ikigai is no longer there. It may simply **be changing shape**.

Doubt is also proof that you are attentive, committed and sincere in your search.

Exercise: dialogue with your doubt

Take a sheet of paper and write at the top:
"Dear doubt, what are you trying to tell me?"

Then let the sentences flow, without filtering them. Write a whole page, as if doubt were writing you a letter.

Then respond to it:
"Thank you. This is how I feel in return..."

This dialogue will help you **better understand what needs to change.**

SHEET 50 – Living your Ikigai means loving being alive

Ultimately, living your Ikigai is not about succeeding at everything, mastering everything, understanding everything.
It is **feeling that your life has flavour, warmth and direction.**
It is loving to get up in the morning, even in the face of uncertainty.
It is being connected to what makes sense to you, in the present.

Living your Ikigai means **loving being alive. Not in a perfect way. But in a true way.**

It is not a goal. It is a way of life.

Ikigai is not a diploma to obtain, a summit to reach or a job to find.
It is an **inner state**, an art of coming to terms with:

Who you are

What you love

What you are going through

What you offer

Every day becomes an **opportunity to live a little more authentically.**

Ikigai does not eliminate storms... but it provides an anchor

There will always be:

Doubts

Fatigue

Crossroads

Losses

But with Ikigai, you have an **inner compass**, a direction to return to.
Even in chaos, a thread connects you to your deepest drive.

To love being alive is...

Feeling joy in simple things

Being moved by a moment of truth

Choosing to nurture what makes you feel freer

Feeling that your life reflects who you are

Savouring, even briefly, the fact of being here

Your Ikigai cannot be defined, but lies in **the quality of your connection to life.**

Exercise: your closing sentence

Take a sheet of paper and complete this sentence without thinking:

"Living my Ikigai is..."

Write down whatever comes to mind. Even if it's simple. Even if it's vague. Even if it's poetic.

Keep this sentence somewhere.
Reread it when you need to.
It is **your truth at this moment**.

Conclusion - A living path, not a set of instructions

You have just explored 50 cards. 50 steps. 50 possible openings to **move towards your Ikigai**.

Perhaps you have applied some of them. Perhaps you have highlighted others for later.
The important thing is not to do everything. The important thing is to **feel that something has been set in motion within you**.

Your Ikigai is not found in a book. It is found in

Your daily choices

Your deepest impulses

Your silences, your intuitions

Your simple joys

Your sincere efforts

What you hold in your hands is a compass

It does not impose a course on you.
It helps you **listen to your own direction** and return to yourself whenever you stray from it.
Ikigai is a path of listening, truth and presence.

An **imperfect but living** path.
An **intimate but universal** path.

And now?

Take a deep breath.
Close your eyes.
Simply ask yourself:
"What would be my next small step in alignment?"

Don't try to do too much.
Just one step. One action. One more accurate word.

This is how Ikigai is lived.

Printed in Dunstable, United Kingdom

71828042R00094